TO WALK IN SEASONS
—An Introduction to Haiku—

AN ANTHOLOGY
(with study guide)
of Japanese haiku in English versions

by

WILLIAM HOWARD COHEN

Charles E. Tuttle Company
RUTLAND, VERMONT & TOKYO, JAPAN

#447470

Representatives

For Continental Europe:
BOXERBOOKS, INC., *Zurich*

For the British Isles:
PRENTICE-HALL INTERNATIONAL, INC., *London*

For Australasia:
PAUL FLESCH & CO., PTY. LTD., *Melbourne*

For Canada:
M. G. HURTIG, LTD., *Edmonton*

Published by the Charles E. Tuttle Company, Inc.
of Rutland, Vermont & Tokyo, Japan
with editorial offices at
Suido 1-chome, 2-6, Bunkyo-ku, Tokyo

Library of Congress Catalog Card No. 72-79016
International Standard Book No. 0-8048-0893-7

First printing, 1972

PRINTED IN JAPAN

For GREGOR SEBBA and

the late

CHARLES V. S. BORST

to whose memory this poem is dedicated

☙❧

Though we are far
and the long night parts us
I still hear your song.

TABLE OF CONTENTS

PREFACE

❦

Much has been written about the difficulty of translating poetry from one language to another. Robert Frost, for example, has said, "Poetry is what gets lost in translation," which is typical of the usual attitude toward translations (although much more clever and direct than the usual comment). Nevertheless, poets over the centuries have continued to translate into their own languages poems that have excited their interest and sensibilities. It is my impression that the best translations, at least from the standpoint of poetry (literal accuracy is another matter), have resulted when the poet wrote a "parallel" poem in his own language based on the original. This assumes that the poet was attracted in the first place because he found in the "foreign" poet a kindred sensibility. This has not always been true, of course, but it has been true often enough to make translation of poetry a "going proposition."

The above is simply stating that these translations are freely made poems based on the originals. In each case the attempt has been to get the spirit and thrust of the original into English (where necessary for the content or humor, American English). My method was to study all the available translations I could in English and then make my own version. Sometimes the latter came after reading only one English version but, where necessary, I changed my first version after reading other renderings. The most helpful books were R. H. Blyth's six-volume study and the works by Harold G. Henderson and the Japanese Classics Translation Committee (see Further Reading, p.97).

In arranging the poems for the anthology, I have given separate sections to the four great masters of haiku: Basho, Buson, Issa, and Shiki. The minor figures, many of whose individual haiku are equal or superior to some by the masters, are grouped together in the last part of the anthology. I have not gone into detail on the history of haiku because this is intended to be an analytical rather than a historical introduction to the form. The best works in English on the history are those by H. G. Henderson and R. H. Blyth.

It will be noted that many of the translations are not in the strict haiku syllable count. There are several reasons for this. In the first place, the Japanese haiku poets themselves have not always followed the 5-7-5 principle. Basho's famous "Autumn Crow" poem, for example, was originally five, ten, and five syllables. In this connection, see H. G. Henderson's *Haiku in English,* and his article in *American Haiku,* vol. 2, no. 2. In the latter he writes,

> . . . the 5-7-5 "syllable count" does emerge as a norm, but *many, many haiku, including some of the most famous of them all, have other counts* [my italics; p. II.]

In the second place, sometimes the Japanese words involved have more syllables than the corresponding English words (e.g., the "Old Pond" haiku of Basho), in which case to fill them out in the translation is to pad the poem and thus destroy the concentration that makes haiku what it is; also in this regard, punctuation in Japanese consists of words whose syllables count, which by itself may add as many as three syllables that in English could not be carried over without padding. Roy Teale, editor of the special issue on Japan of *Literature East & West* (vol. 9, no. 3, September, 1965), points out at the end of the haiku section of that issue that thirteen or fourteen syllables would be closer to the weight of the Japanese poem, because of the difference between Japanese and English syllable-counting discussed by Henderson in his *American Haiku* article. Of course there are times when the English translation must have more syllables than the original haiku.

The above reasons would be enough to justify a translator diverging from the 5-7-5 count, but there is a third justification. If the translator is to make parallel poems out of his translations rather than slavishly literal transcriptions, he must allow the Muse some freedom of movement. Regardless of the surface count, every poem has its own rhythm in the original, and the translator must seek his own rhythm to convey the exact tone with which he was struck when experiencing the original; every poem must be experienced uniquely before it can be rendered in the poet's own language. I leave it to the reader to decide if each haiku has a flavor and rhythm of its own which matches, or reveals more or less, the content of the poem.

On the other hand, I must admit that, as Mr. James Bull, editor of *American Haiku,* has prodded me into accepting and enjoying the challenge of the 5–7–5 norm in my original haiku, I have found my-self (where possible without violence to English and to my experience of the original) translating in the 5-7-5 frame. This explains why many of the follow-ing versions are 5-7-5 or close to it.

As is obvious from the above, I approached these haiku from the point of view of an American poet and not as a scholar. I could not have done it, of course, without the work of the scholars who, to our never-ending debt, have made this great body of poetry available to us.

WILLIAM HOWARD COHEN

Pippa Passes, Kentucky

ACKNOWLEDGMENTS

To Gregor Sebba, distinguished visiting professor of comparative literature at Emory University, who introduced me to haiku and who encouraged me to do my own interpretations.

To James Bull, patron saint of American haiku poets, who by browbeating me in some of his infamous letters made me aware of the high standards involved in haiku and in some of his kind letters inspired me to reach toward them.

To Ping Chia-kuo, professor of history at Southern Illinois University and chairman of the department, who encouraged me to do research on Chinese antecedents to haiku in his superb course on Chinese history, and who provided some of the germinal ideas that appear in my introduction.

To the late Charles V. S. Borst, formerly chief editor of the Charles E. Tuttle Company (Rutland), who was unfortunately killed in an automobile accident during the writing of this work. He believed in this book and, by asking me to write it, is ultimately responsible for its existence.

> Beauty that was has entered everything.
> It has not passed beyond the bounds
>   of being.
> The trees knew it was there; the birds
>   imbibed it.
> Skies curved above it their enduring mantle.
> But greater than all these the world
>   within you
> Grew to a universe bathed in its light.
>
> —W. H. C.

To Sue Brown, secretary to Dr. W. G. Moore, chairman of the philosophy department at Southern Illinois University, who typed the introduction, and to Dr. Moore, a great gentleman and scholar, who did not ever complain about the graduate student who borrowed his "private" secretary.

To Margaret Ackley, secretary to the president of Alice Lloyd College, who typed the anthology with accuracy and loving care.

To Dr. William S. Hayes, president of Alice Lloyd College, who has encouraged me in all my creative endeavors, and put up for some years with a very maverick employee. If he ever gets ulcers, some of them will be my doing.

To *Literature East & West, Haiku West,* and *Twigs* (Pikeville College), in which some of the poems in this volume originally appeared, and to *Haiku Magazine* (Winter, 1970), which published the section of the Introduction on the seasons.

Lastly, because in the end all things come down to her: To my wife, in whose lyrical eyes I try out all my poems.

> Pure lyric were you
> in the sun and all of the flowers
> knew it and were laughing.

INTRODUCTION
—The Nature of Haiku—

BASIC PRINCIPLES

The Japanese haiku is a miniature poem which holds roughly the same place in Japanese poetry that the sonnet holds in English and Western European poetry. It is a three-line poem in which the lines contain five, seven, and five syllables respectively.[1] To this requirement Harold G. Henderson, in his monograph *Haiku in English,* adds three others: the haiku should contain some reference to nature; it should deal with a particular occurrence; and what is going on in the poem should be in the act of happening.[2] There are, of course, exceptions to these "rules" (or principles), but those least violated are the second

[1] See Preface, p.9, on variations from strict syllable count.
[2] New York, N.Y.: 1965. Tokyo and Rutland; 1967 (revised edition).

19

and third. There are a very few haiku that do not deal with a specific aspect of nature.

The haiku, like any good poem, must present experience from a fresh point of view, and in this sense the Japanese haiku is no different from good poetry in any tradition. Where the haiku differs most from Western poetry, of which the English and American traditions are a part, is in its nonintellectuality. A good haiku does not interpret itself by a bald statement of its meaning, but presents what we can call a "pure image," from which the reader is expected to draw out the meaning himself. For this reason the Japanese haiku is the most direct, objective, and highly concrete poetic form to be found in world literature. To put this in another way, it is poetry "stripped to the bone." To the Western reader, accustomed to a more wordy, rhetorical, philosophical type of poem, the haiku often seems fragmentary and incomplete.

Some of this effect is caused by the fact that the haiku was originally the first part of a longer poem, the *tanka* (containing five lines with the syllable count 5-7-5-7-7), or the *renga* (linked verse in which a number of poets wrote alternate poems of three and two lines: 5-7-5, 7-7; 5-7-5, 7-7, etc.). In these forms the haiku (or *hokku*—"starting verse"—as it was called at that time) was the first three-line unit, which established a mood or suggestion that could be further developed in the subsequent links.

However, the fragmentariness of haiku cannot all be accounted for in this way. Many commentators have noted the tendency in Japanese painting, for example, to treat the part in such a way as to suggest the whole. A single shoot of bamboo suggests the entire grove, a single bird the entire sky, a single tree branch all of nature. This ultimately goes back to Chinese brush-painting in which the rhythm of the stroke has maximum suggestive powers and in which empty space is used to suggest large natural forces, such as waterfalls, mountain torrents, the sky, or the sea.

It is hard not to see here also the influence of Zen Buddhism with its emphasis on *satori*, sudden enlightenment, in which in a flash of insight the Zen student realizes his oneness with the universe. According to this tradition, the "Buddha nature" is to be found in all things large and small and wherever it is encountered it is the same indwelling and all-encompassing spirit. The most famous haiku in the literature, *"Furu ike ya,"* known by heart by almost all Japanese, is said to have been composed in this connection. According to one tradition Basho (d. 1694), who is credited with giving haiku its mature form, was sitting in the garden with his Zen "master" (teacher), who suddenly asked him, "How is the Buddha revealed to you, right now?" A frog landed in the pond and Basho answered:

Furu ike ya	Mossy pond;
kawazu tobikomu	frog coming in—
mizu no oto.[3]	splash!
	[my free version]

The answer given by Basho tells more about the essence of haiku than volumes of prose. It reveals that what is going on at a particular moment and in a particular place stands for the whole fabric of reality and the entire life of the universe.

The way in which this poem expresses immediate (direct) awareness or enlightenment (*satori*) should be obvious without analysis. My version differs from others in English mainly in its emphasis on the simultaneity ("nowness") of the poem. Unless the frog is in the act of plunging into the pond I believe the "aliveness" which is the essential flavor of this haiku is lost and the poem becomes something inert and dead. (The other variant in my translation is letting the concrete image "mossy" stand for the age of the pond.)

[3] Literally: Old pond / frog jumps in / water sound.

TECHNIQUES: THE CHARGED IMAGE

Another key poem in the career of Basho is essential to the understanding of what a haiku is. It also illustrates the way in which a single image can sum up a much larger whole. It was written two years before the famous "Old Pond" haiku and, with it, marks the dividing line between Basho's "early" period and his mature style.

> Bare branch
> and a crow balanced on the twilight:
> autumn nocturne.

Another version (though leaving out the word "autumn" to bring out another side of the poem) may help us to see what Basho sought to convey with his imagery.

> When the crow arrives
> on the bare, withered branch
> true night has come.

Of all the haiku written on autumn, a favorite haiku season for all the Japanese poets, this one certainly conveys most fully and completely the somber and melancholy mood of late fall through a single, stark, unforgettable image.

On the basis of the latter poem and the many haiku that follow its method, we can put our fingers on one of the main devices by which the haiku achieves its characteristic effects. This consists of a simple image "charged" with atmospheric, emotional, or "mood" effects. The "charged image" is a way of conveying intense emotional content through a simple objective image. The best way to explain this is to cite distinguished examples of this technique by Basho, perhaps its inventor and certainly its master.

> A lone bird follows
> in this gray autumn
> my darkening path.

> Night falls on the sea—
> the voices of wild ducks
> hazy and white.

> White cherry blossoms;
> white wisp of mist;
> dawn-lit mountains.

One of the most fascinating aspects of haiku that may reflect the influence of Zen Buddhism is the practice of bringing together seemingly disparate elements by showing their hidden or unsuspected unity. Here are some examples by the masters:

> On the wide seashore
> a stray blossom and the shells
> make one drifting sand.
>
> —BASHO

> A flash of lightning
> and the jagged screech of a heron
> flying through the darkness.
>
> —BASHO

> Temple by the sea:
> the breakers pulsing in beat time
> to the holy flute.
>
> —BUSON

> Blooming chrysanthemums
> and this dump heap
> sharing the same landscape.
>
> —ISSA

> The sound of the evening bell;
> the noise of ripe persimmons
> landing in the temple garden.
>
> —SHIKI

The placing side by side of seemingly unrelated elements in many haiku leads us to another technique of the haiku poet, one that we find in poetry all over the world, though in a less concentrated form. By placing two unrelated or even opposed elements in juxtaposition (against each other), the poet is able to reveal completely different aspects of reality. An example from Buson (18th century) will illustrate this.

> Amid the falling
> of honeysuckle petals
> the mosquitoes buzz.

Here something pleasant and something unpleasant are combined and the contrast adds a certain sharpness, and even freshness, to the poem. We are led to experience the honeysuckle from a completely different angle, the angle of the mosquito. He, too, enjoys the flowers, placidly ignoring the fact that we are not accustomed to perceiving him from this vantage point. Some other examples of this technique follow.

> Sharp in the silent evening,
> black in the last green light,
> a bat among willows.
> —KIKAKU

That little willow
braving it out
right next to Mount Fuji!
—ISSA

This bush-warbler dares
to wipe his muddy feet
on my plum-blossom stairs.
—ISSA

Connected with the technique of opposing elements is the method of reversing relationships from
the expected one to one that reveals a wholly new
dimension of experience. A haiku by Basho is an
apt example.

Wild, churning surf—
breaking over the island
the milk-white heavens.

In this haiku the expected reference to the sea
surrounding the island is reversed by the last line,
creating a brilliant and startling effect. When we
know that the Chinese and Japanese refer to the
Milky Way as the River of Stars the reversal then
becomes more understandable but no less exciting
and memorable.

Another example of reversal illustrates a key

aspect of haiku, the transformation of a simple situation by a shift in perspective. For example, Rogetsu, by reversing the time sequence, gives a timeless dimension to a very simple series of events.

> The tree frog's song
> and the young leaves' movement
> completed by the rain.[4]

The phenomenon of reversal brings us to the very heart of the haiku problem: the kind of "logic" that gives haiku its peculiar thrust, its ability to startle us awake to a world in which clarity, mystery, and wonder merge to make the everyday life around us seem as if we have just looked at it for the first time. Despite the disputes as to just how much Zen Buddhism there is in haiku (and we will not attempt to settle the argument here) it is difficult not to associate the flash of insight that comes in reading the best haiku with the Zen concept of *satori* or sudden awakening. (The name "Buddha" means literally "the man who woke up.") Of course one might argue that such an experience comes with all true poetry, whether Oriental or Western, and with this we will not quarrel. Note that in the above examples

[4] The normal sequence would be: first rain, then moving leaves, then frog song.

of reversal, and the ones below, the last line carries
the punch.

> Under the cherry shower
> water down the mountain
> turning stones to songs.
>> —ONITSURA

> Dipping my hands
> in the crystal spring;
> oak leaves shattering.
>> —SOIN

> Sudden spring rain—
> the street now a garden
> of gay makeshift hats.
>> —OTSUJI

> Primal energies
> that broke this stone-piled fence:
> two amorous cats.
>> —SHIKI

THE BUDDHIST PERSPECTIVE

The last two poems above lead us to the subject
of humor in haiku, a very important aspect of the
form. Although it began when the *hokku* was the

first part of the *renga,* or linked verse (which was not much more than a party game played by the lords and ladies at the imperial court), in its mature form it cannot be separated from a basic layer of Buddhism in the Japanese mind; thus the haiku poet tends to see man as simply one more element in nature with no inherent superiority or elevation above any other part. In fact, in Zen Buddhism one often senses that man is considered inferior to the rest of nature on the grounds that he has lost the intuitive spontaneity that he once shared with the animal kingdom. Walt Whitman has expressed this feeling exactly in the "Song of Myself." "I think I could turn and live with animals, they are so placid and self-contained." The whole purpose of the Zen discipline is to lose the feeling of being isolated in the universe and to regain the experience of oneness with all things that the animals have always had, although man seeks it on a higher and more spiritual plane, of course.

One reason why children and young people sometimes are able to write very good haiku almost immediately is that they have yet to lose their natural oneness with and responsiveness to the world around them. The ability to see man as no better than other creatures, or even inferior to them, opens up some wonderful possibilities for humor. Take the following, for example:

I sit like Buddha
but the mosquitoes don't recognize
my Nirvana.

—OEMARU

To have mosquitoes comment on one's spiritual attainment is quite a situation. What can one say about the charm and self-perceptiveness of a people who can be so objective about themselves in the most serious situations? Here are some other haiku which derive their humor from this objectivity:

My neighbor scouring saucepans
and the tree frogs piping—
what a duet!

—ISSA

These perfect morning-glories!
the faces of men are always
a little off.

—ISSA

The island taunts the water,
cool and blue below it,
with one drunken pine.[5]

—SHIKI

[5] Here the island, the pine tree, and the sea are treated as if they were human creatures with personality.

> Daytime frogs cry, "Night!"
> nighttime frogs cry, "Day!"
> only a bunch of grumblers.
> —BUSON

A poem by Issa, probably the greatest humorist among the haiku poets, illustrates this same type of humor, working through the poet's indentification with such creatures as insects and frogs. On a hot summer day Issa was waiting in the antechamber to see an important official on business (he had a long legal fight to claim his rightful inheritance from his father, due to the machinations of his stepmother). Out of this situation he made what I consider one of the greatest of all haiku:

> One man
> and one fly
> waiting in this huge room.

The surface situation of a man, bored by a long and tiresome wait, passing the time by watching a fly go round and round in the room is humorous enough —as well as being quite a universal experience. The fact that beneath the surface humor are all kinds of serious undertones only serves to heighten the humor by contrast, a very typical device in haiku.

This poem alone illustrates just about everything we have said above about haiku. The way it derives from the objective situation is absolutely clear (every good haiku is completely lucid on the surface) and yet the possible deeper levels of meaning are seemingly endless.

A Note on the Variant Translations

The presence of these seemingly endless possibilities makes "translating" or rendering haiku (*translating* suggests word-by-word fidelity which is impossible in poetry) a very intriguing and difficult task. One of the most serious problems, and the one that has caused many poets to denounce the whole idea of translating poems, is that a translation usually loses the overtones, the suggestiveness, the other possible layers or levels of meaning which made the original poem so fascinating. The reason why the best poems can be read over and over is that the different levels that are thus discovered make the poem ever new and the reader more and more aware of and sensitive to the many-sidedness of life and the human mind. Because a translator usually has to decide which of the aspects of the original he is going to concentrate on, he often has to give up any attempt to suggest the other layers of meaning, the other possibilities. One way of grappling with this is doing several different versions of the same poem for the purpose of bringing out a different aspect in each rendering. This enables me to move around in the poem (which ideally is moving around in the original experience on which the poem is based) and to have, so to speak, a "conversation" with the poem or the author.

In the case of the famous "Autumn Crow" haiku discussed in the first section of this introduction, I made the first version to emphasize the visual aspect of the poem.

> Bare branch
> and a crow balanced on the twilight:
> autumn nocturne.

In this first version it is hoped that the reader will see the leafless branch and the crow silhouetted sharply against the sky at autumn dusk. A second version is:

> When the crow arrives
> on the bare, withered branch
> true night has come.

This was made in an attempt to emphasize the

time aspect of the haiku and the human feeling that comes from the concatenation of two stark, late autumn objects, and nightfall (the momentary fusion of space and time?).

A third rendering, reducing the poem to a minimum, probably brings it closer to the sparseness that is the essence of haiku in the Japanese, although for a Western audience a slightly expanded translation doubtless seems more natural because we are accustomed to longer poems.

> Barren branch;
> balancing crow;
> autumn dusk.

This suggested exercise for the reader of haiku might prove enjoyable and lead to a deeper understanding of its nature. He might take one of the poems in the Anthology and make his own version or versions. One method is to see how far the haiku can be reduced to its barest essentials. A second "translation" might then be made to bring out some overtone or suggestion found in the Anthology version or suggested by the situation in the poem. This would yield a minimum and a maximum version of the poem.

For example, the version of Basho's "Old Pond"

haiku above (Mossy pond; / frog coming in— / splash!) is an attempt to make the simplest, most direct, most concrete translation possible. Two variations below suggest the kind of thing that can be done by expanding an idea hidden or suggested in the poem.

> When the old pond
> gets a new frog
> it's a new pond.

Explaining this will probably kill it, but the purpose was to suggest the "Buddhist enlightenment" (*satori*) aspect of the original. It was inspired by the statement of one of my Kentucky-mountain students that "the frog landing in the pond is Buddha landing in the mind." (They had just been introduced to the Buddhist background of haiku.) According to the tradition, when Buddha "woke up" he was sitting under the bodhi tree in what, as many Japanese haiku poets have suggested by their frog poems, was something like a frog's natural position.[6] (I remember when I was in Korea in 1947 being amazed by the length of time that Asians could squat on their haunches.)

[6] Thus frog on a lily pad is equivalent to Buddha on the Lotus Throne.

Just recently I tried a version that handles the same poem like a *koan*, a Zen Buddhist spiritual puzzle used by masters to drive their students out of abstract thinking into direct awareness. As Paul Reps has said in *Zen Flesh, Zen Bones*, a collection of koan, these puzzles "don't make sense; they make you."[7] Here is the poem:

> The bungling frog
> leaped for the pond, but landed
> in Basho's brain.

This may be a little tricky, but it suggests some of the fun that can be had "moving around" in a haiku to test some of its other possibilities. This is also to probe some of the creativity of one's own mind. As some poet said long ago (was it Basho?), "a good haiku poem is like a finger pointing at the moon"; once you have seen it you don't need the finger. Perhaps for each person there is a different moon that corresponds to his own vision, temperament, and imagination. Thus, making one's own versions could be a way of gaining one's own understanding of self and universe, a way of letting oneself in on the poem of life.

[7] See for Further Reading, below, p.98.

TIME AND ETERNITY: THE SEASONS

This brings us to an interesting and fundamental problem, the seasonal word or element that is supposed to be in every haiku. In the early centuries of haiku the seasonal element, one of the most superficial aspects of the genre, was emphasized. Whole dictionaries of season words and phrases were published to insure "correctness" in this regard: "the moon" means the full moon of autumn, but "the hazy moon" means spring; and so on. As with many other aspects of the form, it was Basho who saw and developed the profounder possibilities of the seasonal element. He achieved this in two ways, by making it a matter of inner mood and atmosphere rather than surface imagery or verbal tricks and by giving it a Zen Buddhist flavoring in the sense of an encounter between time and timelessness. A good example to illustrate both is the following haiku about an abandoned temple:

> The stone gods vanished—
> only the dead leaves kneeling
> on this temple stoop.

Here we have a powerfully evoked image of late autumn which at the same time reveals the eternal truth that all things, even the gods, are swept away into the endless void. Note that the eternal element is gone and the momentary element—the leaves—remains. The mood and atmosphere of the season are completely objectified by the image, which yet can, upon reflection, make a profound statement about life.

Some other examples:

> White, sifted mountain
> reverberates in the eyes
> of a dragonfly.[8]
>
> —ISSA

> Immortal Fuji
> rising so lonely there
> no leaf can fall on you.[9]
>
> —BUSON

[8] This beautifully evoked encounter between the tenuous and the permanent recalls the Buddhist idea of the unreality of the visible world, in that the great mountain exists momentarily in the insect's eye even as the great world exists in the mirror of the mind for the brief instant that is life.

[9] Here the mountain is a symbol of eternity taken over from Taoism and Chinese Buddhism—the World Mountain; its immunity from the falling of autumn leaves gives it a peculiar loneliness associated with autumn: a very interesting and unusual example of reversal.

Tree of thin tracery—
as leafage now
only the myriad stars.[10]

—SHIKI

Ending this introduction with a discussion of the seasonal aspect of haiku brings us back to the point where we began, the charged image. As seen above, the seasonal mood and the encounter of time and timelessness give to the haiku image a profound suggestiveness, setting the mind on a journey into the universe and through the universe into itself. In the best examples, the perfect meeting of the objective and the subjective imprints the world on the mind and the mind on the world.

[10] This is an image of winter and a juxtaposition of the season-bound tree with the relatively changeless heavens.

THE ANTHOLOGY
—Conversations with the Sages—

In the midst
of the cherry blossoms
there are no strangers.

—ISSA

芭　蕉

BASHO (1644–94)

Early in his life Basho became a retainer of a samurai family and with his noble companion Sengin
studied haiku under the master Kigin. On the death
of Sengin, Basho, deeply stricken, at the age of
twenty-five left feudal service for the life of a more
or less itinerant poet-monk, earning his living as a
teacher of *renga* (linked verse) and haiku. Many of
his students became well-known haiku poets, and
his reputation as a teacher equals his reputation as a
poet. His great travel books and his haiku poems
reveal him as one of the most appealing personali-
ties in world literature as well as the greatest poet
Japan has produced. The fact that he was able to
establish himself as a major figure in world literature
on the strength of his work in such a restricted form
as haiku indicates his power, as well as the possibilities
of the form.

Spring has come with the mist
to honor you with a new cape,
gray nameless mountain.

Village without bells—
what do they listen for
in the spring evening?

Mountain road—
sun rising warm
into the plum scent.

White cherry blossoms;
white wisp of mist;
dawn-lit mountains.

How many flowers
are blossoming in the mind
when the cherry blooms?

After the bells
had sung their song, the flowers
rang with fragrance.

Fancy butterfly
perfuming her wings floating
over these blossoms.

What myriad worlds
are created now
by these cherry blossoms!

Each bloom that falls
creates all over again
the spring universe.

"Only to grow here!"
the leaves say, the buds say,
reflecting the sun.

Standing their ground here
the tender and green leaves
glow in the sunlight.

Mossy pond;
frog leaping in—
splash!

Never to forget
the delicate savor—
life's fragile dewdrop.

Wide seashore—
a spray of bush clover,
shells, and drifting sand.

Since there is no rice
into the bowl
go flowers.

How to say goodbye!
so like a bee who would stay
all day in one flower.
[composed on leaving the house of a friend]

The Mogami River
washing this steaming day down
into the sea.

The rain is falling
but the hollyhock
still points to the sun.

Although this skylark
sings the whole day long
his throat still feels cramped.

In the rainy dusk
the flamboyant hibiscus
makes its own sunset.

All around this stillness—
but one sharp locust scraping
breaks the rocks in two.

Echoes of the bell
following the misty paths
of autumn dawning.

One flower unknown
to bird and butterfly blooms
in the autumn sky.

In the autumn sky,
its birds and its clouds,
I feel my old age.
    [written two weeks before his death]

Brown discarded leaf
clinging tightly
to this green mushroom.

Through a gray forest
I see the sweet bird of dawn
fading in autumn dusk.

Autumn twilight road
made only for the passing
of lonely men.

Tremble O tomb!
as from my wailing throat
this wind of autumn.
    [composed at the grave of a poet friend]

Lovely moon on high—
but when the clouds obscure it
necks enjoy the rest.

Bare branch
and a crow balanced on the twilight:
autumn nocturne.

Night falls on the sea—
the voices of wild ducks
hazy and white.

A flash of lightning
and the jagged screech of a heron
flying through the darkness.

The stone gods vanished—
only the dead leaves kneeling
on this temple stoop.

All we need is scent
to make these fluffy snowflakes
into flower cups.

Absorbing the rush sparrow
into itself, the willow
sleeps on there.

Empty vase, empty sky,
full sakè cup
and a lone drinker.

Between love and barley rice
the lady cat
is growing lean.

After I watched the moon
its departing shadow
followed me back home.

Wild, churning surf—
breaking over the island
the milk-white heavens.

蕪　村

BUSON (1715–83)

Buson was a famous painter as well as a poet, and his visual sensitivity is readily apparent in his mastery of poetic imagery. Because of his painter's eye, Buson brought a piercing objectivity and concreteness to haiku poetry. He is one of the best haiku poets to study for the qualities of lucidity and surface clarity. Little is known about his personal life.

Plum-blossom river—
how can these reflections
ever flow away?

Plum tree on the fence
throwing its petals equally
on both sides.

Just at the end of spring
this old cherry tree
begins to bloom.

The cherry bloom has fallen
revealing a temple
rising between the trees.

Poor empty twigs—
all you are good for now,
to gather fallen petals.

Under the blossoming pear
a moonlit woman
reading a faded letter.

Where is the poem
you should have sent in answer?
Lady, spring is gone.

Daytime frogs cry, "Night!"
nighttime frogs cry, "Day!"
only a bunch of grumblers.

Still, breathless noon—
beyond the blossoming fields
the booming surf.

In the evening breeze
the heron ignores the water
lapping on his legs.

Amid the falling
of honeysuckle petals
the mosquitoes buzz.

The rise and fall
of green ocean sighing;
green echoing trees.

Late evening meadow
balanced between the rising moon
and the setting sun.

Moon going up
but how many leaves setting
with the falling sun?

Axe far in the woods
and this noisy woodpecker
hacking away outside.

I could not go in
but had to bow before
this autumn-leaf temple.

Geese calligraphy
on the pale print of foothills—
the round moon a seal.

Immortal Fuji
rising so lonely there
no leaf can fall on you.

Temple by the sea;
the breakers pulsing in beat time
to the holy flute.

一　茶

ISSA (1762–1826)

In humor and sympathy for all that lives, Issa is unsurpassed in the history of Japanese literature and perhaps even in world literature. His sad, underdog life (see the introduction to *The Year of My Life,* Berkeley, 1960) did not defeat him. Instead it afforded him an unusual vantage point, an opportunity to see the world from underneath. He always gives us a unique perspective, an odd angle that provides delight and surprise at every turn.

This bush-warbler dares
to wipe his muddy feet
on my plum-blossom stairs.

In the midst
of the cherry blossoms
there are no strangers.

These perfect morning-glories!
The faces of men are always
a little off.

Ah look! my little hut
has a new blue roof.
What morning-glories!

A dewdrop world
hanging suspended in the dawn
and yet, and yet . . .
    [on the death of his infant daughter]

My neighbor scouring saucepans
and the tree frogs piping—
what a duet!

The old, plump bullfrog
held his ground and stared at me—
what a sour face!

Sometimes the farmer
looking at his scarecrow
almost believes.

Waving the radish
he has just pulled up
he points out the road.

Walking to Shinano
this mountain weighs on my back
in the stifling heat.

Watch where you're going,
boisterous flea! One more jump
and you're in the river.

White, sifted mountain
reverberates in the eyes
of a dragonfly.

Patient woodpecker—
evening, and you are still knocking
at the same spot.

One man
and one fly
waiting in this huge room.

The bridge is gone—
O well! I'll have to watch the moon
on some other mountain.

Even when the heart
is slowly dying
the flowers still bloom.

O former tenant,
I know all, all you felt here
down to my frozen toes.

子　規

SHIKI (1867–1902)

Shiki was perhaps the greatest of haiku critics. Like Buson, he strove mightily for objectivity in his haiku, and it should come as no surprise to us that he championed Buson over Basho as the greatest haiku poet. Prolonged illness toward the end of his life gave to some of his work an almost painful hyper-sensitivity. As haiku editor of one of Japan's leading newspapers and as editor of *Hototogisu* (Cuckoo), the leading haiku magazine of the late 19th and early 20th centuries, he was a major influence on haiku during the early modern period. His books on haiku are known to all literate Japanese. Despite some extreme opinions, such as his rejection of Basho, his theories are validated by the fact that his poems based on these theories have given him an undisputed place, with Basho, Buson, and Issa, as one of the four great haiku poets Japan has produced.

I could not see
the departing bird;
plum petals shaking.

Blue April ocean—
over still white mountains, wings
of black homing birds.

Between the bean rows
scattered clumps of lilies;
that's prosperity!

The temple Buddhas
staring out
at the June sea.

All around
this tumbledown house,
perfect morning-glories.

Primal energies
that broke this stone-piled fence:
two amorous cats.

Empty road ahead
after the fireworks—
"Look! one star glides down!"

The island taunts the water,
cool and blue below it,
with one drunken pine.

To write this night
how many insects
dissolved in the ink?

The sound of the evening bell;
the noise of ripe persimmons
landing in the temple garden.

Tree of thin tracery—
as leafage now
only the myriad stars.

Blue twilight ocean
and the islands out there
blossom with new lights.

The red berries
make bright footprints
on the dust of snow.

Under this village
lost in the snow
I still hear the stream.

OTHER POETS

The fact that the poets included in this section have
written some of the finest individual examples of
haiku should be encouraging to us ordinary mor-
tals. Take, for example, Onitsura's singing stones;
Kikaku's "ceremonial cranes," willow-framed bat,
and air-cooling star; Hokushi's movable moon;
Boncho's sun- and tree-grappled eagle's nest;
Kyoshi's dewy-eyed snake or Hashin's snow-can-
celed universe; and Oemaru's mosquito-canceled
meditation. These superb poems by so-called minor
poets give hope to us all.

智　蘊

CHIUN (15th century)

On the edge of the stream,
not knowing its name,
this weed flowers.

貞　德

TEITOKU (1570–1653)

When the world blossoms
it can never be put back.
How the petals fall!

立　圃

RYUHO (1595–1669)

After the moon and cherry blossoms
having lingered in this world,
I know what comes next.

[death verse]

Having seen
the moon and the flowers,
now for a colder beauty.

[alternate version]

遅　望

CHIBO (17th century)

Even the sparrows
can hardly lift their feet
in the hot sand.

宗　因

SOIN (1604–82)

Dipping my hands
in the crystal spring;
oak leaves shattering.

Wild geese writing
their way across the sky;
what a jagged script!

⧄

越　人

ETSUJIN (d. 1702)

Bathed in such flowers
how would it be to die
in these dreamlike hours?

季 吟

KIGIN (1623–1705)

The grass, bending,
waves to the rhythm
of the October wind.

凡 兆

BONCHO (d. 1714)

Sun dropping down
behind a dead tree, whose limb
grasps an old eagle's nest.

In this sudden hush
the scarecrow, toppling, falls
on the empty ground.

素　堂

SODO (1641–1716)

It rained last night
but the fat melons
have already forgotten.

❧

尚　白

SHOHAKU (1649–1722)

The void echoes;
the cuckoo's cry
cancels the world.

言　水

GONSUI (1650–1722)

All that's left of the gale
that died away last night—
this roaring sea.

去　来

KYORAI (1651–1704)

This whole field of frogs
croaking like mad
suddenly stops.

Only a migrating bird,
I sleep like a traveler
in my own village.

千　那

SENNA (1651–1723)

Now no more flowers;
where I looked before
only green leaves.

೧೨

来　山

RAIZAN (1653–1716)

Women planting rice;
all about them muddy
but the clear song they sing.

嵐　雪

RANSETSU (1654–1707)

Making no noise,
eating the rice plant—
a caterpillar

One leaf falling
and then another;
the wind takes all.
[death verse]

∫

許　六

KYOROKU (1655–1715)

The first thing down
when the autumn storm winds blow—
this scarecrow.

北　枝

HOKUSHI (d. 1718)

Taking it off, putting it on,
I tried the moon
on every branch of this pine.

~

其　角

KIKAKU (1660–1707)

Stiffly ceremonial
the tall cranes parade
in the New Year dawn.

Who could wake the gardener
on this misty morning—
cherry blossoms falling?

Sharp in the silent evening,
black in the last green light,
a bat among willows.

All things made cool
while falling on Musashi plain
this white, cold star.

鬼　貫

ONITSURA (1660–1738)

Eyes go one way;
nose goes another;
and flowers come in spring.

Under the cherry shower
water down the mountain
turning stones to songs.

However we call
the firefly goes
its own way.

The day has gone
in waves of heat
up on the mountain.

When the cool breeze comes
the roof of the sky resounds
with pine-tree voices.

Who could keep
his brush away
from this moon tonight?

丈　草

JOSO (1661–1704)

No snow as cold
as this winter moonlight
on my whitening hair.

露　月

ROGETSU (1666–1751)

The tree frog's song
and the young leaves' movement
completed by the rain.

浪　化

ROKA (1672–1703)

The snow fell last night—
today a cold blue heaven
and white-dusted pines.

                         ☙

巴　人

HAJIN (1676–1742)

Tell me this silence
that spreads with the moonlight,
saucy cicada.

春 郊

SHUNKO (18th century)

A booming waterfall
beside this mountain path
mocks at the heat.

∞

召 波

SHOHA (d. 1771)

The silent grass answered
the rumbling of the wagon
with one butterfly.

太　祇

TAIGI (1709–72)

How about that cat
purring under the eaves
in the swirling snow!

∽

大江丸

OEMARU (1719–1805)

I sit like Buddha
but the mosquitoes
keep biting.

I sit like Buddha
but the mosquitoes don't recognize
my Nirvana.
　　[alternate version]

閑　更

RANKO (1726–99)

On the bare twilit shore
the fishermen unload
strange watery treasures.

☙

士　朗

SHIRO (1742–1813)

Are they clouds
rising behind that hedge?
Or plum blossoms?

成 美

SEIBI (1748–1816)

Someone has stepped
onto the wooden bridge—
every frog is still.

The cold, rainy day
makes these scarecrows
share our human fate.

可都里

KATSURI (d. 1817)

Out to look at snow—
stragglers disappear in mist;
only I am left.

芭 臣

HASHIN (b. 1864)

The sky is gone
and the earth is gone
but the snowflakes still are falling.

⁓

小　波

SAZANAMI (b. 1870)

This heavy snow
and the heaving sea;
how quietly they fuse.

虚　子

KYOSHI (b. 1874)

The snake went on
but left its dewy eyes
shining in the grass.

∽

乙　字

OTSUJI (1881–1919)

Sudden spring rain—
the street now a garden
of gay makeshift hats.

鞍　風

[dates unknown for the following poets]

AMPU

The skylark's voice
absorbed everything;
even the spaceless void.

∽

真　原

MAHARA

The sea bird
and his shadow
meet at the curve of the sea.

Swooping up and down
the seagulls ride the currents
of the wild surf.

玄 駛

GENSHI

I watch the bamboos
looking for motion. . . .
O this heat!

❧

可 幸

KAKO

Through this steaming day,
carrying his load of wind,
the fan seller.

STUDY GUIDE

A NOTE ON THE STUDY OF POETRY

Of all the arts, none is so easily killed as poetry when subjected to an inappropriate method of study. Since all art involves variety in unity, poetry can be studied and analyzed, but, like all art, any good poem is much more than the sum of its parts. Recalling the old poetic saying quoted in the Introduction, a good poem is a finger pointing at the moon, but one must not mistake the finger for the moon. So the analyzable parts of a poem are fingers pointing to the totality of the poem, but it is these elements in their active and total inter-relation that make it a living entity. (Rather than teach dead poetry it is better not to present it at all.)

There is another problem involved in the teaching of poetry which is a pedagogical one. When students are plunged too quickly into an exhaustive analysis of poems they are apt to back away in frustration. "But I didn't see all that when I read the poem," they are likely to say. "If poetry is that complicated it is beyond me." So it is better to lead gradually into analysis, beginning with fairly obvious surface elements and only later leading into more subtle and complex aspects. A further dividend from this method is that the student may himself learn to find his way from the surface elements in the poem to the deeper, more fundamental ones. And this after all is what education is all about. If we provide exhaustive analysis right at the beginning, we make the student a cripple, ever after looking for some scholarly précis to copy from a book.

SUGGESTED SEQUENCE OF STUDY

To help the beginner in discovering haiku for himself, I would suggest the following sequence of study:

1. After reading the minimum definition of haiku in the first paragraph of the Introduction, read randomly* and see if you can notice key haiku elements. Some questions that may be helpful at this point are: How are these poems different from familiar Western poems? What is the effect of their brevity? Is there a typical imagery and, if so, what is it? How is it different from or similar to familiar Western imagery? Can you discern any differences in the styles of the various poets? If so, what are they?

*A number of recent researchers have demonstrated that random learning is the most efficient kind, a paradox until one remembers some of one's own magical, completely independent discoveries.

2. Read the first series of haiku quoted in the Introduction (p. 23). The "charged images" in these haiku convey "intense emotional content through a simple objective image." What aspect of the imagery is emotional? How does the *objective* image become *subjective* (personal) because of the particular angle of focus involved in each poem?

3. Read the second series of haiku in the Introduction (p. 25). In these haiku seemingly disparate elements are brought together by "showing a hidden or unexpected unity between them." How is this done? Are the relationships really there or are they provided by the mind and imagination of the poet? If the latter, do you discern any differences in the methods used by each poet to relate these disparate elements? Look through other poems by these poets in the Anthology. Are these methods followed in their other poems? How? Try to write at least one haiku (do not worry about the syllable count when first starting out) in which you relate seemingly unrelated objects or images. After writing it you can try to revise it for 5–7–5-syllable lines. Start by looking out the window and listing the first things you see (very quickly and without too much thought); then try to relate those that have the least surface connection.

4. The poem by Issa on p. 32 of the Introduction is a good illustration of the relationship between surface image and underlying meaning in haiku. Try to show how the underlying meaning derives from the image in this poem.

5. Read the section of the Introduction called "A Note on the Variant Translations" and try making your own version or versions of one of the poems in the Anthology, first reducing the poem to its barest essentials, and then trying to bring out some overtone or suggestion omitted in the first version.

FURTHER READING

Amann, Eric: *The Wordless Poem.* Box 866, Station F., Toronto, Canada.

Basho (Matsuo): *The Narrow Road to the Deep North and Other Travel Sketches.* Edited and translated by Nobuyuki Yuasa. Penguin Books: Baltimore, 1966.

Blyth, R. H.: *Haiku.* 4 vols. Hokuseido Press: Tokyo, 1949–52.

———: *History of Haiku.* 2 vols. Hokuseido Press: Tokyo, 1963–64.

Bull, James, and Spiess, Robert, eds.: *American Haiku.* Formerly published three times a year at Box 73, Platteville, Wisconsin, this major outlet for American haiku poets and critics is out of print now but available in libraries.

Cohen, William Howard: "The Calligraphy of the Cosmos: The Essence of Haiku," *Literature East & West*, vol. 9, no. 3. Modern Language Association of America: New Paltz, N.Y., September, 1965.

Haiku Society of America Newsletter. Haiku Society of America: New York, N.Y.

Haiku West. Ed. Leroy Kanterman. Japan Society: New York, N.Y.

Henderson, Harold O.: *Haiku in English*. Japan Society: New York, 1965. Charles E. Tuttle Company: Tokyo and Rutland, 1967 (Revised Edition). By joining the Japan Society, 250 Park Avenue, New York, N.Y. 10017, one can obtain material on Japanese culture.

———: *Introduction to Haiku*. Doubleday-Anchor: Garden City, New York, 1958.

Ichikawa, Sanki, ed.,: *Haikai and Haiku*. Nippon Gakujutsu Shinkokai (Japan Society for the Promotion of Science; Japanese Classics Translation Committee): Tokyo, 1958.

Issa (Kobayashi): *The Year of My Life*. Edited and translated by Nobuyuki Yuasa. University of California Press: Berkeley, 1960.

Reps, Paul: *Zen Flesh, Zen Bones*. Charles E. Tuttle Company: Tokyo and Rutland, 1957.

Stewart, Harold: *A Chime of Windbells: An Anthology of Japanese Haiku*. Charles E. Tuttle Company: Tokyo and Rutland, 1969.

———: *A Net of Fireflies: Japanese Haiku and Haiku Paintings*. Charles E. Tuttle Company: Tokyo and Rutland, 1960.

Watts, Alan: *The Way of Zen*. Viking Press: New York, N.Y., 1960.

Yasuda, Kenneth: *The Japanese Haiku: Its Essential Nature, History, and Possibilities in English*. Charles E. Tuttle Company: Tokyo and Rutland, 1957.

INDEX OF HAIKU POETS

99

Other TUT BOOKS

Botchan by Soseki Natsume; translated by Umeji Sasaki

The Buddha Tree by Fumio Niwa; translated by Kenneth Strong

Comrade Loves of the Samurai by Saikaku Ihara and **Songs of the Geishas** translated from the Japanese by E. Powys Mathers

The Counterfeiter and Other Stories by Yasushi Inoue; translated by Leon Picon

Exotics and Retrospectives by Lafcadio Hearn

Five Women Who Loved Love by Saikaku Ihara; translated by William Theodore de Bary

A Flower Does Not Talk: Zen Essays, by Abbot Zenkei Shibayama of the Nanzenji

Folk Legends of Japan by Richard M. Dorson

Gleanings in Buddha-Fields: Studies of Hand and Soul in the Far East, by Lafcadio Hearn

Harp of Burma by Michio Takeyama; translated by Howard Hibbett

Historical and Geographical Dictionary of Japan by E. Papinot

A History of Japanese Literature by W. G. Aston

TUTTLE BOOKS ON HAIKU

A Chime of Windbells: A Year of Japanese Haiku
by Harold Stewart

A Net of Fireflies: Japanese Haiku and Haiku Paintings
by Harold Stewart

The Japanese Haiku: Its Essential Nature, History, and
Possibilities in English, with Selected Examples
by Kenneth Yasuda

Haiku in English (revised edition)
by Harold G. Henderson

Like Haiku: Haiku, Tanka, Other Verse *by Don Raye*

Typhoon! Typhoon!: An Illustrated Haiku Sequence
by Lucile M. Bogue

Borrowed Water: A Book of American Haiku
by the Los Altos Writers' Roundtable

Pageant of Seasons *by Helen Stiles Chenoweth*

Haiku of Hawaii *by Annette Schaefer Morrow*

Alaska in Haiku *by David Hoopes and Diana Tillion*

Charles E. Tuttle Company

PUBLISHERS